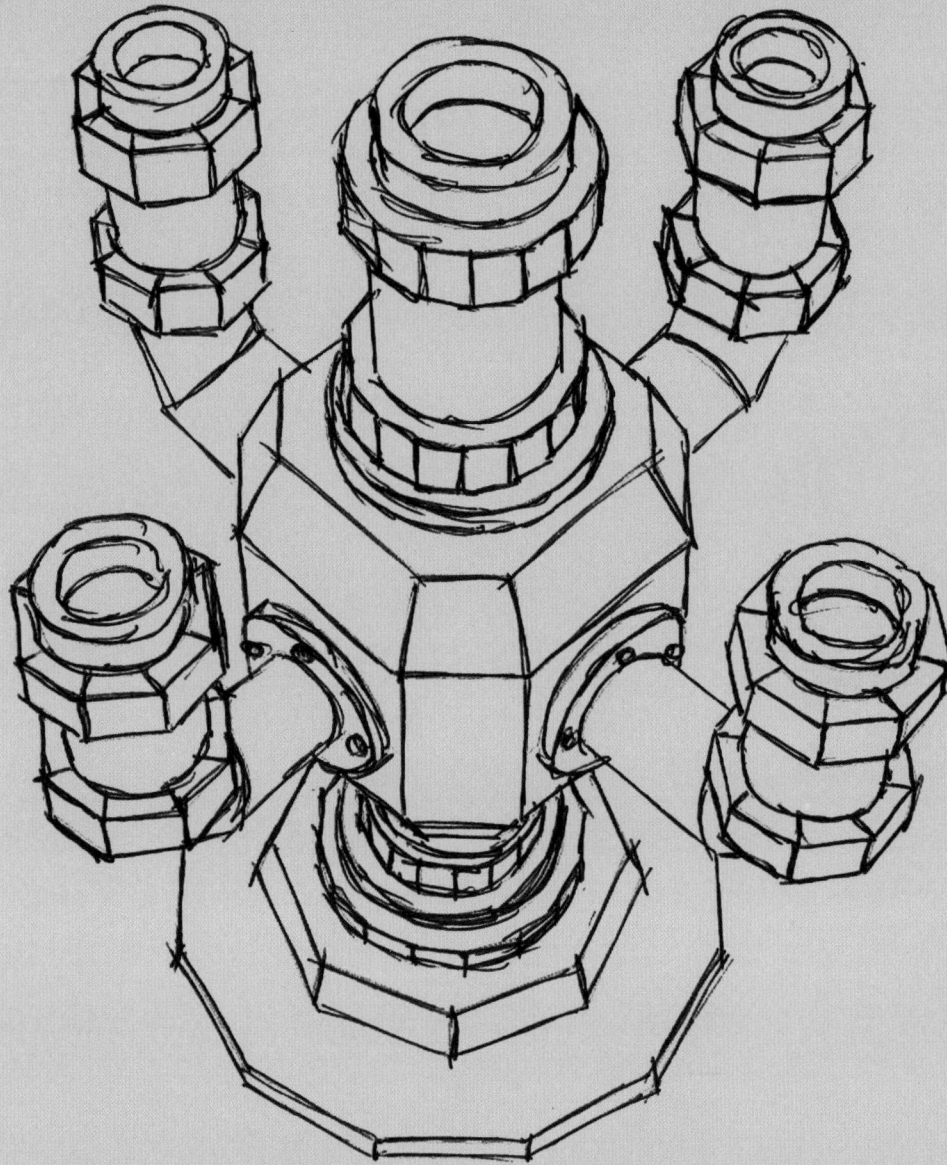

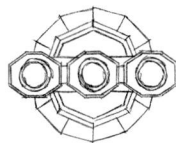

Aerial Media Company (2016)
in collaboration with WOTH

AART VAN ASSELDONK

DESIGNER OF
THE MIRACULOUS

TABLE OF CONTENTS

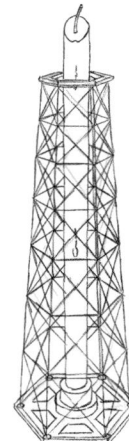

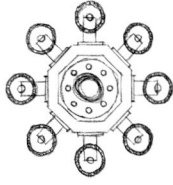

1

WORKSHOP

THE FOUNTAINHEAD

Since 2008 Atelier of Aart van Asseldonk is based in a mishmash
of a tool sheds and outbuildings behind the house of his parents.
Aart feels best at home in his workshop, surrounded by the flat
Kempen countryside in the south of The Netherlands. This is the
place where he first discovered his love for engineering, taking
apart a moped engine or a brand new radio when he was 'playing
around, curious to see how things work'. After finishing
secondary school and a few courses at St. Lucas vocational
college in Boxtel and Mechelen Art School, Van Asseldonk
was accepted at ArtEZ, the Arnhem Art School. There, Wilma
Sommers, head of the 3D Design department, took the kind of
hands-on approach that immediately appealed to him. Sommers
(1960-2012) was a strong, quirky personality who – under the in-
fluence of punk counterculture – had embraced the profile of the
self-producing designer in her own practice. As a senior lecturer,
Sommers radically steered away from the Modernist axiom of
teaching design as a course specifically in preparation
for a career in the industry. Her perspective was informed
by the sober reality of the Dutch situation of the eighties and
nineties; the industry had moved out and jobs offers slacked
off. Meanwhile the growing popularity of design studies at
ArtEZ and Eindhoven AIVE* called for a new curriculum: one
that prepared students for an independent multi-disciplinary
practice. Sommers, an open-minded yet demanding teacher,
encouraged Aart van Asseldonk to convert his inborn passion
for craft and mechanical ingenuity into a consistent portfolio
of objects. Van Asseldonk energetically worked his way through
art school with his friend and ally Pim Wetzels: 'In retrospect,
we owe much to the philosophy and art history classes taught
by Margriet Hovens. She helped us find our direction and,
more importantly, incorporate the right words into presenta-
tions'. In 2008 a wooden model of Heat Stove 01 successfully
crowned Van Asseldonk's graduation portfolio at ArtEZ

Two versions of the Trouble
Light (2013) and some parts
on the table. In the background a series of studies for
new objects in the Allegory of
the South (2015)

The workshop of his father
Arie van Asseldonk, a
specialist building contractor,
houses the thriving Atelier
van Asseldonk since 2008.

HEAT

'Beating and grinding the metal
into the desired form we burn our
eyes sore and sometimes even risk
to loose a finger or two'.

Aart van Asseldonk loves to work
in precious oak and walnut to
produce refined objects like
Trouble Light, Unimate (2013)
and Time is Ticking (2015). This
preference stems from his father
Arie, whose furniture is stacked in
the back (right).

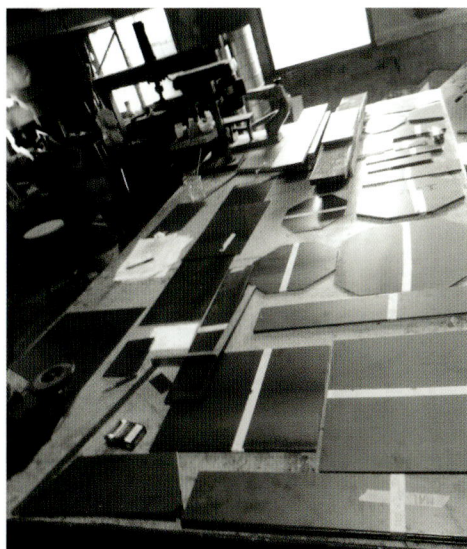

DETAILS

A selection of geometrically shaped parts of sheetmetal are sorted on a table. After a proces of welding and sanding it finally results in the monumental three-armed Flare Stack for De Waag in Leiden. (2015)

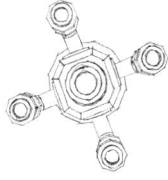

4

FLARE STACK

MONUMENTAL PRESENCE

'Burning gas shooting through high factory chimneys and large plumes of fire bursting into the air... As a young kid I was fascinated by the contour of those flames against the evening sky when we drove past the petrochemical refineries south of Maastricht'. By far the most literal adaptation of the industrial flare is Heat Stove 02, although the memory of the flames on top of a chimney also gave impetus to the design of the large blue Flare Stack, which later developed into four variations. The prototype was first presented by invitation from Maarten Baas as part of his Side Show exhibition during the Salone del Mobile 2014. The stove was a prominent feature of the small exhibition, its boldness standing in stark contrast to precious objects like the Unimate and Trouble Lights. Flare Stack stood alongside Heat Stove 01 because the two objects shared a similar monumentality, although the candelabrum makes a more playful statement. Enhanced by its dark blue skin, roughly-welded joints and large bolts, the sheer expressiveness of the object visually claimed the space surrounding it. Exaggeration of size and emphasis of the skin of the object blends the definitions of modern sculpture and architecture into the realm of design. Like the Trouble Light, the Flare Stack gradually grew into a collection in which different materials and sizes were explored. The smaller version of the Flare Stack in oak shows great refinement of surface, which emphasizes the geometrical composition of circles and angular bodies.

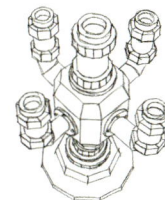

Over the years, Flare Stack has appeared in different sizes and materials like deep blue steel, dark oak, walnut and zinc.

The dark colour of the four-armed candelabrum (134 cm) was achieved by submerging the object into heated waste oil.

Meticulous craft and deep understanding of the material draws attention to the geometric composition of octagons, decagons, dodecagons, circles and columns.

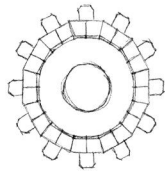

5

EXPERIENCE THE KEMPEN

BELEEF
DE KEMPEN

136

NO 81

TAKE A HIKE

Vessem is an ancient village in the vicinity of Eindhoven. It grew up around a crossing of roads near the Beerze brook and was officially granted municipal rights in 1292 by Duke John I of Brabant. The landscape of this region offers a rich variety of oak woods, bog and heath, which appeal to hikers. To stimulate this type of environmentally friendly tourism Vessem commissioned a project called Beleef de Kempen (Experience The Kempen) and appointed Aart van Asseldonk to come up with a suitable plan. The Kempen strays over the border into Belgium (like Brabant itself) which, in the old days, stimulated the rise of a cunning guild of smugglers running their illegal merchandise over a network of small forest trails. Van Asseldonk focused on the old border stones and cast iron posts that were the indicators of the boundaries in this region. The basis of his way-finding system was a network of newly designed concrete columns that mark the routes. At the starting point of the walk, a general map shows an overview and visitors walk between the columns describing the particular coordinates of the place in corten steel. The system was accompanied by an Experience The Kempen app for iPhone.

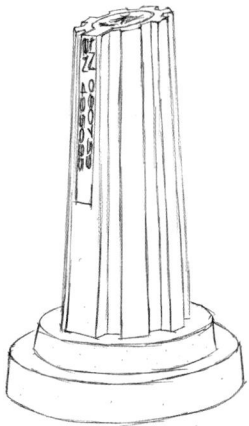

The new ribbed column on a round base really stood out because of the strong contrast between the light concrete and the corten steel indicating the precise geographical coordinates of the point.

Van Asseldonk took reference from cast iron ornamented posts that previously scattered the landscape of this region between Holland and Belgium. The app, map and columns made up a navigation system to help visitors enjoy their walk around a network of trails in the Kempen countryside around Vessem.

NO
BL
55
1
49
13
7

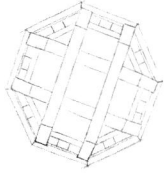

6

TROUBLE LIGHT
& UNIMATE

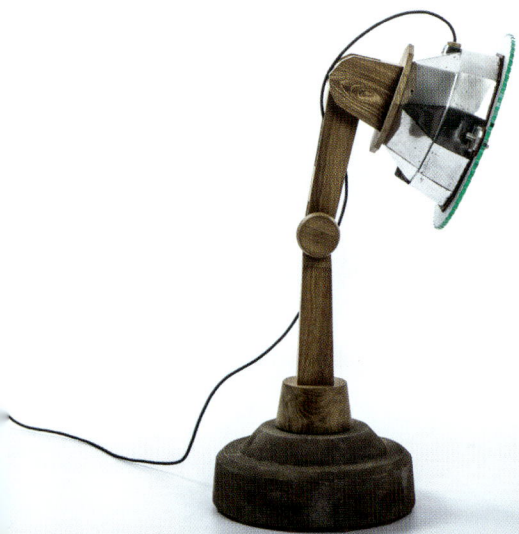

1977
2014

8

CHV NOORDKADE

CHV

FANTASY OBJECTS

In 2014, a group of local entrepreneurs in Veghel started an initiative to revive some of the cultural and social importance held by CHV, the largest producer of cattle feed in Europe, before the factory closed its doors in 2010. Situated along the Noord-kade (North Quay) this occupied a series of large buildings and formed the core of the economic and industrial welfare of the region. The new enterprise, named CHV Noordkade, commissioned Aart van Asseldonk to come up with five centrepieces to herald the re-opening of the large factory hall. To make a metaphorical connection between the new, mainly culture-oriented ambitions and the heritage of the place, he took remnant artefacts from the abandoned factory and assembled them into fantasy objects. The archaeology of the CHV premises richly provided all kinds of bits and pieces like a porcelain insulator and a large wooden box, and also a beautiful palette of colours and the pleasing angular shapes of the transformers. Using these items, Van Asseldonk constructed a generator, a bridge, a crane, a large crate and tower and a 'vault for the factory director'. Strange contraptions such as these, which in their appearance only hint at certain prototypes and serve no other use than to entice the imagination, are typically called follies. His Modern Times project in Eindhoven and the experience on the large scale of CHV Noordkade, certainly gave Van Asseldonk momentum for his later work Allegory of the South.

'The Box' is one of a series of five follies that Van Asseldonk assembled from parts found at the derelict CHV factory.

'THE BRIDGE'

It looks like a triumphal arch.
The name, like the object itself
poses the visitor with a riddle
and stirs the imagination.

LAMP ON A CRANE

A Trouble Light hangs from a
pulley attached to a shack.
It resembles an old harbour
crane, but lacks a rail carriage
and doesn't have a proper mast.

BOX AND TABLE

A visual riddle to stir the
imagination: a large wooden
crate with a table on one side
and a steel box on a small
tower on the other.

A DIRECTOR'S VAULT

A strong box without a
lock is ironically called
'the directors vault'.

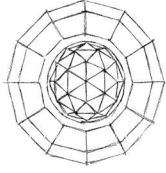

9

FORMWORKS

FLAT-PACKED ENTERTAINMENT

Elevated chimneys have developed into a genre in Van Asseldonk's portfolio. The first model (Heat Stove 02) stands on a tubular construction which lifts the hearth off the ground, and is surrounded by concrete benches that retain heat and offer people a warm place to sit. Apart from its symbolism as a nostalgic reference to an industrial age, the elevated chimney also ensures effective combustion. Van Asseldonk used his experience of the one-off design of Heat Stove 02 to develop Form Works, which is intended as a commercial product for use in private gardens or public spaces. Form Works is a hearth surrounded by a shelf, which is not intended as a seat but which can be used to rest your feet or to keep your tea warm. Its brown rusty corten steel skin blends in easily with most natural surroundings – especially on summer and autumn nights, which probably are the perfect occasions for a family to gather around the outside stove. As part of social entertainment Form Works is also a highly visible centrepiece. The articulation of the ribs make Form Work a sturdy stove. As the name implies, Van Asseldonk based the rib design on formworks which are used in the building industry to cast concrete. More than form alone, they are also used to bolt the circular elements of the stove together. Because it can be delivered as a construction box, Form Works turns the monumental into a viable commercial product.

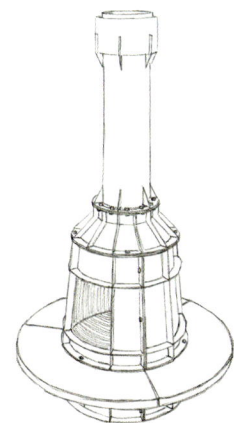

The expressiveness of
Form Works is also part of
the functionality. It can be
delivered in parts, which are
then bolted together.

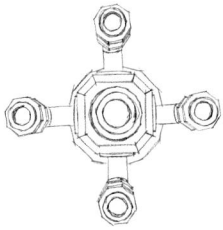

10

DE WAAG

UNDERSTANDING ARCHITECTURE

In 2015 De Waag, a new café and restaurant, opened in a prominent monument in Leiden. De Waag was built in 1657 to a design by Pieter Post, a well-known master of Dutch Classicism. He was also the architect of Huis ten Bosch, now a royal residence in The Hague. Pieter Post envisioned the weighing house in the centre of Leiden as a simple square block. Clad in ashlar stone, the facade has a relief sculpture by Rombout Verhulst, proudly illustrating the weighing that went on inside over the centuries. In 2014, its purpose sadly reduced to the merely ornamental, hotel and catering entrepreneur Debuut proposed an ambitious conversion of the building into 'the new living-room for Leiden'. This was not a simple refurbishment of course, but a building process fraught with problems stemming from the clash between the demand for modern comfort and the strictest regulations for a 17th century grade 1-listed monument. Van Asseldonk became involved in the final stages of the interior design when he was commissioned to produce a customised Flare Stack candelabrum. Due to the strict fire regulations, the bio-ethanol fluid that was used in earlier models of the Flare Stack was replaced by an evaporator that emits harmless water vapour, as well as yellow and orange lights to simulate flames.

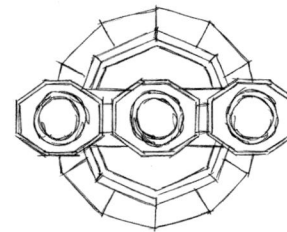

CANDELABRA

The simple, bulky, three-armed
Flare Stack commands a strong
presence in the room, achieved by
its monumental size and elevated
position on a pedestal (which dou-
bles as a cabinet, also designed
by Van Asseldonk). This is further
reinforced in subtle details: the
matte finish, octagonal shape and
the end pieces of the burners,
which all cleverly echo the architectural columns in the space.

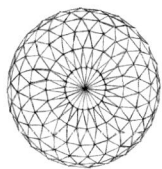

11

SHISH TABLE

The shish table was a visitors' favourite during the Focolare exhibit at Plus Design gallery during Salone del Mobile 2015. After the show it was bought by a shish lounge in Dubai.

STEP INTO THE CIRCLE

While the It's Healthy to Piss Out the Fire candelabrum drew inspiration from classical Roman architecture, the World Gathering Table, which was also presented at the Focolare expo at Plus Design, reinterpreted the shish water pipe. Generally associated with meeting places in the Middle East, water pipes have been growing in popularity amongst European youngsters in recent years. According to Aart van Asseldonk, it needed a little update for the 21st century, however, so he came up with a new model, supported by a specially designed table. 'Roundness permits an equal position for every user and makes it a truly democratic model'. His walnut table and pipe were built up from clean circular and angular parts, just like earlier designs such as Heat Stove 01 and Flare Stack. In this item, cultural connotations of form play a more prominent role. A circle stands for the universal need for cosiness, comfort and social interaction. By changing the central piece on the table, the user can adapt the setting to suit local tradition: a samovar makes it typically Russian and a Lazy Susan automatically making it the scene of a Chinese restaurant. This shish is a highly stylized architectural fantasy, connecting the outline of a minaret to a domed renaissance baptistery.

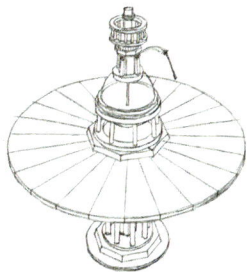

The walnut pipe is a folly, entertaining a likeness to architecture from the Middle East, the renaissance and even fantasies represented in Hieronymus Bosch's painting The Garden of Earthly Delights (ca. 1480-1490).

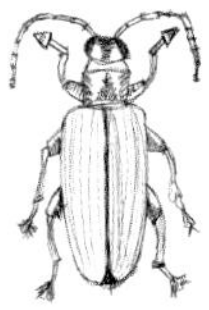

12

TIME IS TICKING

HOW LONG WILL IT LAST?

Traditionally a clock is an ornament, elegantly reflecting the owner's taste. The Time is Ticking tells a different story: a golden pedestal reminds us of a glorious past, whilst wormholes show the decay of its wooden case. A real beetle – not the usual miniature brass eagle, globe or unicorn –crowns the top. In Van Asseldonk's version, nature itself is teaching us to embrace a different and more honest approach to beauty. The bugs have to be kept isolated, hence the bell jar and a remote winding mechanism hidden in the pedestal. Together with Wageningen University, Van Asseldonk researched how many woodworms it would take to devour the wooden casing in eighty years (which reflects the average life expectancy of an owner). When the timepiece drops from the demolished casing, it causes the connection to the winding mechanism to break and stops the clock. In this work, popular advertising claims like 'this product will last you a lifetime' are juxtaposed to the biblical aphorism 'Vanity of vanities! All is vanity', which points to the shallowness of things that are not what they seem and do not perform what they promise. The concept of vanitas was often depicted in 17th century still-lives, showing skulls, withering flowers, soap bubbles, overturned glasses, decayed books and clocks.

13

SAFE STORAGE

NOTHING SLICK HERE

This outsized Safe Storage cupboard was a central piece in
the Modern Times exhibition at the 2013 Dutch Design Week.
Van Asseldonk specifically wanted to design an oversized
bulky object that opposed and exaggerated the slickness of
contemporary cabinets. It was one of the boldest contrapositions
against the slick perfection of contemporary furniture as there
ever was. The overwhelming and voluminous cupboard took its
basic angular shape from 17th century iron mills; a large central
pavilion supported by ribbed buttresses on each side. Keeping
with the character of the Modern Times exhibit, it was all
tongue-in-cheek. The sheer size and power of Safe Storage
completely denied it the kind of functionality one would
normally expect from a cupboard. Instead, all the components
of the object – its size, sound and technical solutions – were
exaggerated and designed to bedazzle. By turning a large steel
wheel in the centre, visitors were able to open the mysterious
vault. The resistance of the bulky valve was accompanied by
the loud grinding of 25 gears, which immediately captured
the attention. It seemed to take ages to unveil the contents of the
safe. Finally, instead of revealing a treasure chest of high-end
design, the vault opened up to reveal a rather bland cargo
of books and a stack of wooden cases.

DISFUNCTIONAL

Pure fascination for the
ingenuity of transmissions
prompted Van Asseldonk to
design a perfect disfunctional
gearbox that emitted loud
rumbling noise and produced
a lot of counterbalance to delay
the opening of the vault.

14

THE ALLEGORY OF THE SOUTH

A LANDSCAPE OF FOLLIES

'You really blew everyone's mind this time,' a thrilled
Maarten Baas exclaimed when he first set eyes on the Allegory
of the South. Maarten Baas, already an established name in
the international design scene, was first captivated by Aart van
Asseldonk's original approach in Modern Times of 2013.
Some months later, Baas generously promoted the younger
designer's second presentation at the Salone del Mobile 2014
in his Side Show. Aart van Asseldonk needed every ounce of his
natural charm in order to launch the first stages of the costly
and daring project around mid 2015 and gain the endorsement of
companies in the Eindhoven region. He invited the support of the
best tradespeople in the south of Holland: the imaginative flower
arrangements were done by Oogenlust and all the constructive
sections of the fantasy architecture were made and mounted by
specialist exhibition builder Bruns. A small regional brewery,
Beerze Beer, also supported the project, whilst the catering was
taken care of by chef Dick Middelweerd of De Treeswijkhoeve.

TATTOO CARPET

Tattoo artist Bob Geerts designed several carpets adapting iconography quoting objects like 'It's healthy to piss out the fire' and others referring to Bruegel and Bosch. The carpets were produced and sponsored by Brunschot Projects, Oirschot.

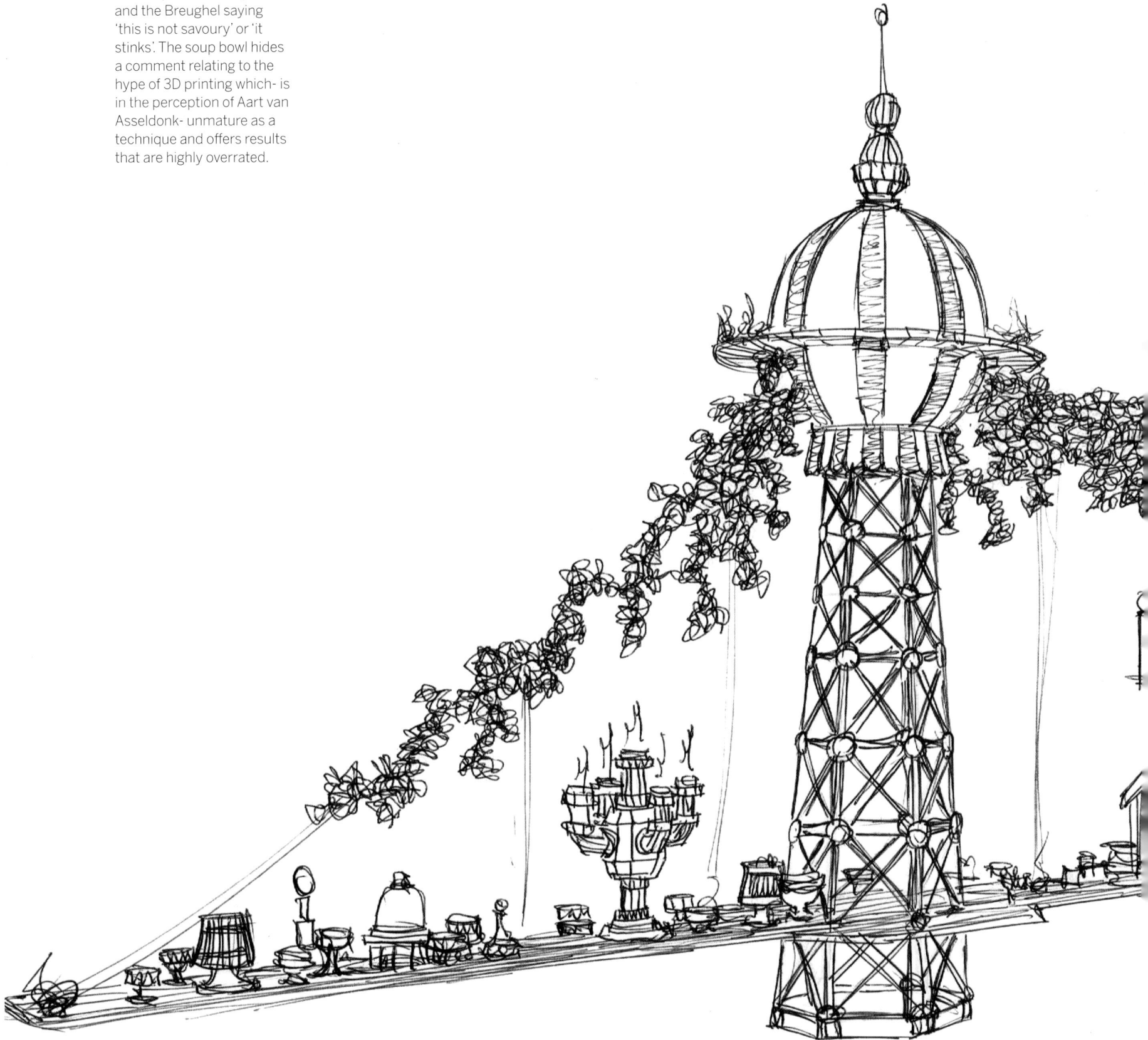

Left page The plastic soup bowl in the centre stands out between the more fancy objects. It's form refers to an antique chamber pot and the Breughel saying 'this is not savoury' or 'it stinks'. The soup bowl hides a comment relating to the hype of 3D printing which- is in the perception of Aart van Asseldonk- unmature as a technique and offers results that are highly overrated.

PRELIMINARY STUDY

A festive landscape of
architectural contraptions
and guirlandes, shown here
in a preliminary study. Like
some other items, the array
of chairs and stools were not
finished on time for the final
presentation.

TABLE PIECES

Right page The Allegory of the South consisted of five main follies that filled the central nave of the church. The event was open to visitors of Dutch Design Week during the day and functioned as a popup restaurant at night. To accommodate guests for the diner (€ 150 each), long tables and benches were placed on the church floor, underneath the follies. Tables were decorated with flowers, arranged by Oogenlust. A collage of pictures and drawings hanging on a door of the Atelier offers insight into the sources of the particular items in the Allegory (page 17). The larger flower arrangements hanging in between the follies f.i. was based on an old black and white photograph of a wedding cake. Another part of the event gave room to an exhibition of objects by Van Asseldonk and some of his proteges. Objects like It s Healthy to Piss Out the Fire, the Wheel of Fortune and the iconography on carpets designed by Bob Geerts were direct transformations of proverbs from the Netherlandish Proverbs, a painting by 16th century painter Pieter Bruegel The Elder. A panorama photo of the Silver Chamber at the Habsburg court in Vienna gave inspiration to the precious table pieces. Other, geometric compositions were derived from a 18th century painting showing vases and pinnacles in a cabinet of curiosities. Finally some others were found by Van Asseldonk in the background of the centre panel of The Garden of Delights by Hieronymus Bosch.

DESIGN CHURCH

In terms of content and scale, projects like Modern Times and CHV Noordkade preluded the highly ambitious Allegory of the South project, presented during Dutch Design Week 2015. To host this larger-than-life project, Aart van Asseldonk persuaded the Augustinian Fathers to lend him their parochial Church of the Holy Heart in the centre of Eindhoven. In the central nave of this 19th century Neo-Gothic church he inserted a breath-taking landscape of follies, taking inspiration from classic works by Hieronymus Bosch and Pieter Breughel The Elder. The Allegory of the South was the talk of the town, probably because unlike other shows in Eindhoven, it steered clear of the expectations of an exhibition of modern design. Five architectural assemblages followed the upward movement of the church's nave: a lighthouse topped by a doghouse, a chapel on stilts connected to a wooden water tank, a windmill spinning like crazy and a metal structure crowned by a wooden platform and a golden dome. The ebullient composition was brought to life by exquisite garlands of purple orchids and green foliage. Awed visitors were seated at oak tables and treated to a pop-up version of De Treeswijkhoeve, a famed two-star Michelin restaurant in nearby Waalre. This tableau of flowers, food and the sheen of perfectly designed objects offered a totally new, bewildering experience.

Alex Munsters, a student at ArtEZ regularly works at the Atelier since 2014. He designed and handmade this series of shoes adapting elements like the socks from examples depicted on 16th century paintings. The items were exhibited on pedestals throughout the Allegory and symbolically referred to Dutch proverbs like 'A Shoe on One Foot, the Other Bare' and 'Jumping into Seven Trenches at the Same Time'.

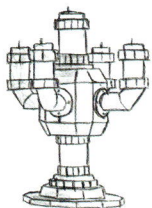

COLLABORATION

Van Asseldonk has started
collaboration with Pols Potten
to produce small items like the
miniature version of a flare stack
serving as a candle stick.

NOODUITGANG

BRVEGEL 1559

FIDES

fides maxime a nobis conseruanda est praecipue in religionem, quia deus prior et potentior est quam homo

A drawing by Pieter Bruegel
The Elder 'Belief' or 'Fides'
(1550) from the collection of
the Rijksmuseum Amsterdam.

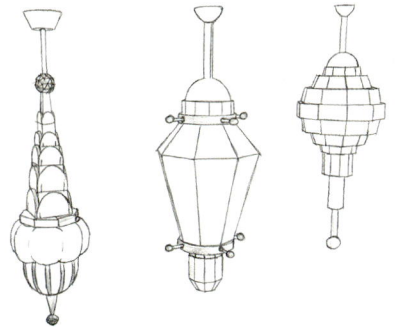

STAR CHEF

Chef Dick Middelweerd (middle)
heading the kitchen brigade
in the Augustinian church,
temporarily turned into a pop
up version of De Treeswijkhoeve
during Dutch Design Week.

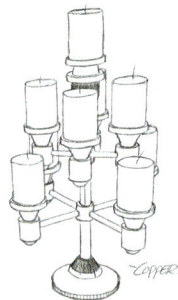

Arie van Asseldonk inspecting the Augustinian church in Eindhoven, prior to the large scale intervention by his son for Dutch Design Week 2015.

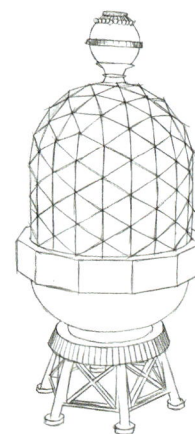

LARGER THAN LIFE IMAGINATION

In this genre picture Aart van Asseldonk is a depicted
as the striking personality that attracts people with his
larger than life imagination. The Art of Persuasion proved
helpful indeed. To realize the large scale Allegory of the
South, Aart needed to engage a group of experienced and
strongly opinionated entrepreneurs to take part and invest
substantially; fltr. Marcel van Dijk flower designer and
owner of Oogenlust, chef Dick Middelweerd of restaurant
De Treeswijkhoeve, Jan Burgmans CEO of Bruns exhibition
builders, Ivo Kaanen of brewery Beerze Beer with partner
Jasper Langenhoff in the window left.

RENAISSANCE MAN

In 2016- on the brink of international breakthrough-
Aart van Asseldonk remains the prototype of the common sense
Dutch designer. Of course; he likes the rock and roll of Milan
and loves to be part of the international scene. Still, within the
realm of his workshop, he follows his own intuition, calmly
deciding what to create and undertake next; however estrange
his choices may drift him away from the newest trends. It is his
love for craft that relentlessly drives him into imagining and
making stoves, candelabras, flare stacks and oil burners.
They function perfectly and startle the imagination. The
monumental sizes and unorthodox combinations of materials
celebrate the riches of the mechanical age; the robust beauty
of industrial materials like steel and the ingenuity of gearboxes,
clocks and pulleys. The aspirations represented in
his larger-than-life objects over the past three years gradually
developed into a kind of fantasy-architecture. In projects like
Modern Times and Allegory of the South Aart van Asseldonk
created a new type of follies based on utilitarian architecture
and the visions of 16th century painters Hieronymus Bosch
and Pieter Breughel The Elder. The contraptions mixing parts
of windmills, watertanks, lighthouses and chapels evoke a rich
world of strange and enticing forms: Aart van
Asseldonk's designs of the miraculous.

RESUMÉ

1984   Aart van Asseldonk is born in Mariaheide, near Eindhoven

2004   St Lucas Industrial and Product Design, MBO
(intermediate vocational education level)

2008   ArtEZ Hogeschool voor de Kunsten Bachelor's degree,
Industrial and Product Design

2010   Amsterdam Fashion Week, sunglasses for the collection
of fashion designer Nicolaas Gerritsen

2010   Dutch Design Week Eindhoven, launch of first collection
ao. Heating Stove 01 and series of furniture at Klok-
gebouw Strijp-S, Apple Store, Conceptstore Kalmoesplein
and MAGDA fashion wear

2011   Concept image and branding 'Slokdarmfestival/
Gorge festival'

2013   Launch Modern Times at Ventura At Work,
a group exhibition in Ventura Lambrate during
Salone del Mobile Milan

2013   presentation of Modern Times at Ketelhuisplein, during
Dutch Design Week Eindhoven

2013   Design CHV De Noordkade at Veghel

2014   Side show presentation of Trouble Light, Heating Stove 01
and Flare Stack Steel in co-operation with Maarten Baas
and Bas den Herder productions

2014   presentation of Trouble Light, Heating Stove 01 at
WOTH- One Week Department Store, during festival
Designkwartier The Hague

2014   presentation of Flare Stack and Form Work part of
'Open Mind' exhibition at The New Kazerne during
Dutch Design Week Eindhoven

2014   designs tables and stools for Coffeelab Eindhoven

2015   presentation of Flare Stack Oak, It's healthy to piss out the
fire and Shish Table at Gallery Plus Design Milan, during
Salone del Mobile

2015   presentation of Trouble Light, Time is Ticking at
WOTH- One Week Department Store, during festival
Designkwartier The Hague

2015   designs a custom made version of Flare Stack for
Restaurant De Waag, Leiden

2015   The Allegory of the South is presented in the Augustinian
church Eindhoven during Dutch Design Week

For Coffeelab, a
coffee concept store in
Eindhoven, Van Asseldonk
designed a series of
workstools and tables,
using steel, smoked oak
and patinated copper.

ACKNOWLEDGEMENTS

Cover image   Gijs Spierings
Back cover   Bas van Poppel
All sketches by Aart van Asseldonk

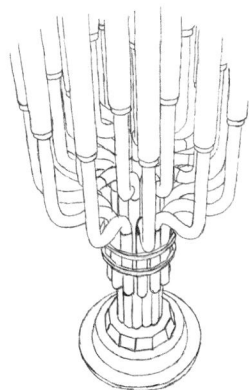

Photo's

Page 2 – 6   Gijs Spierings
Page 11   J.W. Kaldenbach
Page 12   Gijs Spierings
Page 13   Aart van Asseldonk
Page 14   Bas van Poppel
Page 16   Bas van Poppel
Page 17 – 18   J.W. Kaldenbach
Page 19   Gijs Spierings
Page 20   J.W. Kaldenbach
Page 21   Bas van Poppel
Page 22   Gijs Spierings
Page 23   Black and white photo by Aart
                  van Asseldonk, colour J.W. Kaldenbach
Page 24 – 28   Gijs Spierings
Page 29   Johan Nieuwenhuize
Page 30   Gijs Spierings
Page 32   Bas van Poppel
Page 33   Gijs Spierings
Page 37   J.W. Kaldenbach
Page 38 – 44   Gijs Spierings
Page 46   Johan Nieuwenhuize
Page 47 – 62   Gijs Spierings
Page 63   Dennis Brandsma, styling Rob Jansen
                  in collaboration with Perscentrum Wonen.
Page 64 – 66   Gijs Spierings
Page 67   Bas van Poppel
Page 69   Souraya Hassan – Studio Binti Home
Page 70 - 99   Gijs Spierings
Page 101 - 105   Henny van Belkom
Page 107 – 125   Gijs Spierings
Page 126   J.W. Kaldenbach
Page 128 -145   Gijs Spierings
Page 146   Drawing Geloof/Fides by Pieter Bruegel
                  The Elder (1559) from the collection of
                  the Rijksmuseum Amsterdam/Rijksstudio
Page 147 – 153   Gijs Spierings
Page 155   J.W. Kaldenbach
Page 156 – 160   Gijs Spierings

The workshop of his father
Arie van Asseldonk,
a specialist building contractor,
houses the thriving Atelier van
Asseldonk since 2008.

CREDITS

ISBN 9789402601404
NUR 656

A WOTH – Wonderful Things – production

Text: Toon Lauwen
Creative director: Mary Hessing
Art direction: Swan Lian Kwee
Final editing: Rachel Lancashire
Image editor: Beldan Sezen

© 2016 First published in hardback by Aerial
Media Company, Tiel, The Netherlands

The moral right of Aart van Asseldonk and
the photographers to be identified as the
artist and photographers of this work has
been asserted in accordance with the Copyright, Designs and Patents Act of 1988.

www.aartvanasseldonk.com
www.woth.co
www.aerialmediacom.nl
www.facebook.com/Aerialmediacompany

Many thanks to:

Anne van Asseldonk, Arie van Asseldonk,
Hennie van Asseldonk, Els van Asseldonk,
Maarten Baas, Pascal Bastiaans,
Bert van Boxmeer, Fieke van Boxmeer,
Adrie van Brunschot, Jan Burgmans,
Andrea Caputo, Martijn Cimmermans,
Marcel van Dijk, Sherman Emmers,
Bob Geerts, Ties van der Heijden,
Bas den Herder, Jeroen Jansen, Ivo Kaanen,
Jasper Langenhoff, Max van der Louw,
Appie Louwers, Luca Martinazolli,
Dick Middelweerd, Alex Munsters,
Bas van Poppel, Stefan Rovers,
Pierre Stikkelbroeck, Mariëlle van Tol,
Pim Wetzels.

Aerial Media Company bv.
Postbus 6088
4000 HB Tiel, The Netherlands

All rights reserved
No part of this publication may be repro-
duced, stored in a retrieval system, or
transmitted in any form or by any means,
electronic, mechanical, photocopying,
recording, or otherwise, without the prior
permission of both the copyright owner
and the above publisher of this book.
Every effort has been made to obtain
permission for the placing of photographs
from the copyright owners in accordance
with legal requirements. We apologize in
advance for any unintentional omissions
and would be pleased to insert the
appropriate acknowledgement in any
subsequent publication.

Aerial

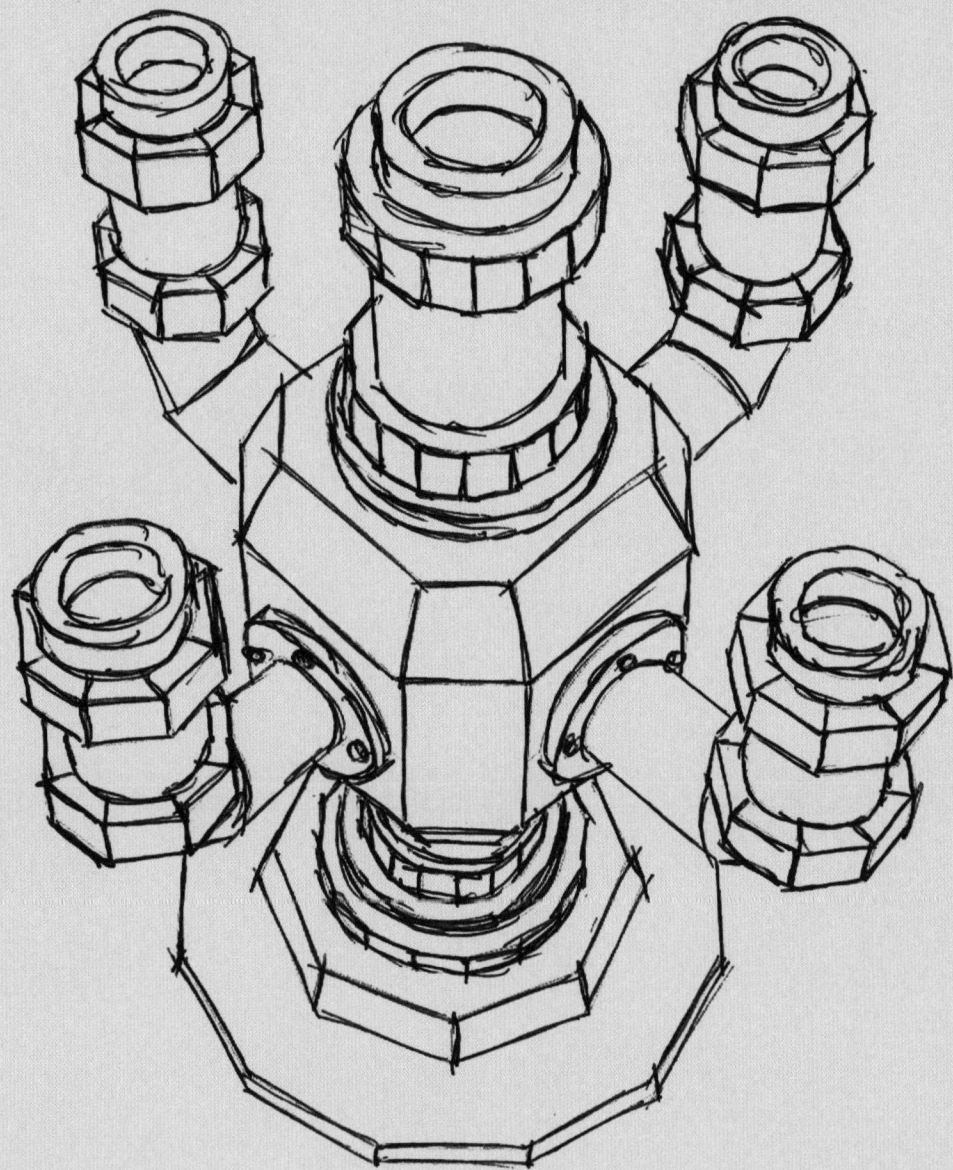